Good Morning, Moroni

Good Morning, Oliver Family!

[signature]

JED NELSON PLATT

Illustrated by SARAH RICHARDS SAMUELSON

[signature]

Published by
Steepleview Studios
Provo, Utah
www.steepleviewstudios.com

Illustrated by Sarah Richards Samuelson
Book design: Eden Graphics, Inc. • www.edengraphics.net
Library of Congress Control Number: 2017941234

ISBN: 978-1-60645-186-1 Paperback
10 9 8 7 6 5 4 3 2 1
First Printing

To Camilla,
and everyone who welcomes Truth

Come ye, and let us go up to the mountain of the LORD . . .
and he will teach us of his ways, and we will walk in his paths
Come ye, and let us walk in the light of the LORD.

ISAIAH 2:2–5

In the tops of the mountains
There is a fountain
And a garden of flowers

And a House with—

Towers

And a gold angel
with glad tidings

Guiding

HOLINESS TO THE LORD
THE HOUSE OF THE LORD

Through big doors
Across polished floors

Are hymns humming along

And oxen holding strong

And youth willing
And spirits waiting

And a grand staircase
And a woman
    with a small suitcase

And a fair-haired man on a chair
And a person in prayer

And a bride and groom

And a family in a special room

And windows of light

And white

And a celestial chandelier

And Father near

There is joy around
And peace inside

Good morning, groom
Good morning, bride

Good morning, Moroni
way up high

Good morning, youth
full of truth

Good morning,
those I cannot see

Good morning,
forever family

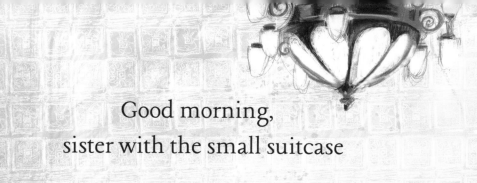

Good morning,
sister with the small suitcase

Good morning,
brother with the smiling face

Goodbye, noise

Goodbye, rush

Good morning, Spirit
whispering "hush"

I commend you
us of whom
I apostles have
he grace of God
also the Lord
he Holy Ghost,
a record of
em, may be and
be in you. Amen
—Moroni

Good morning

Good morning

Welcome home

Doctrine & Covenants 128

Now, what do we hear in the gospel which we have received? A voice of gladness! A voice of mercy from heaven; and a voice of truth out of the earth; glad tidings for the dead; a voice of gladness for the living and the dead; glad tidings of great joy.

How beautiful upon the mountains are the feet of those that bring glad tidings of good things, and that say unto Zion: Behold, thy God reigneth!

And again, what do we hear? Glad tidings from Cumorah! Moroni, an angel from heaven, declaring the fulfilment of the prophets.

Ephesians 2:19–22

Now therefore ye are no more strangers and foreigners, but fellowcitizens with the saints, and of the household of God; And are built upon the foundation of the apostles and prophets, Jesus Christ himself being the chief cornerstone; In whom all the building fitly framed together groweth unto an holy temple in the Lord: In whom ye also are builded together for an habitation of God through the Spirit.

Malachi 4:6

And he shall turn the heart of the fathers to the children, and the heart of the children to their fathers, lest I come and smite the earth with a curse.

1 Corinthians 15:29

Else what shall they do which are baptized for the dead, if the dead rise not at all? Why are they then baptized for the dead?

Matthew 16:19

And I will give unto thee the keys of the kingdom of heaven: and whatsoever thou shalt bind on earth shall be bound in heaven: and whatsoever thou shalt loose on earth shall be loosed in heaven.

Doctrine & Covenants 109

That all people who shall enter upon the threshold of the Lord's house may feel thy power, and feel constrained to acknowledge that thou hast sanctified it, and that it is thy house, a place of thy holiness

That all those who shall worship in this house may be taught words of wisdom out of the best books, and that they may seek learning even by study, and also by faith

And that they may grow up in thee, and receive a fulness of the Holy Ghost, and be organized according to thy laws, and be prepared to obtain every needful thing

And that this house may be a house of prayer, a house of fasting, a house of faith, a house of glory and of God, even thy house

That thy servants may go forth from this house armed with thy power, and that thy name may be upon them, and thy glory be round about them, and thine angels have charge over them

And from this place they may bear exceedingly great and glorious tidings, in truth, unto the ends of the earth

Thank you, Moroni

Although you lived a solitary life, you now stand in golden glory
as a beacon of gathering—pointing us to our heavenly home.
You are the messenger of hope and restoration. Your eternal vigilance
assures all who heed the words of truth the promise of a good morning.

Temples I Have Visited:

_____   _____

_____   _____

_____   _____

_____   _____

_____   _____

_____   _____

_____   _____

_____   _____